encountering Jesus

20 Guided Meditations on His Life and Teaching

encountering Jesus

Patty McCulloch, MHSH

ave maria press Notre Dame, Indiana

www.avemariapress.com

International Standard Book Number: 0-87793-713-3

Cover design by Brian Conley

Cover photo: www.comstock.com

Text design by Katherine Robinson Coleman

Printed and bound in the United States of America.

Library of Congress Cataloging-in-Publication Data
McCulloch, Patty.
Encountering Jesus : 20 guided meditations on his life and teaching /
Patricia McCulloch.
      p. cm.
      Includes index.
ISBN 0-87793-713-3 (pbk.)
1. Jesus Christ--Biography--Meditations. 2. Catholic
youth--Prayer-books and devotions--English. I. Title.
BT306.43 .M33 2001
232.9'01--dc21

                                      2001002526
                                          CIP

contents

introduction

PLACING YOUR SELF INTO THE SCENE.

IMAGINING THE PEOPLE.

SEEING THE SIGHTS.

FEELING THE ATMOSPHERE.

RELAXING INTO THE MOMENT.

Without a doubt, guided imagery is a wonderful way to pray. All you need to find is a quiet place, space to relax, and freedom to allow the imagination to work. When I have led both teenagers and adults in this style of prayer I have witnessed profound moments. Those who are usually assertive and loud learn to still themselves and enter into an encounter with God. Others who are shy and reserved use their natural instincts to express their faith. I have been surprised to hear what these pray-ers have seen and heard in their meditations. They talk about actually encountering God. I have learned to trust that God meets them—as he does for all of us—right where they are.

This book is intended to bring you into twenty scenes with Jesus. These scenes cover a full range from Jesus' life, from his early life, through some of the main teachings of his ministry, to events surrounding his passion and resurrection. For most of their lives, Catholics young and old have heard stories about Jesus. However, with guided meditations they have the opportunity to put themselves into the story. These are encounters whereby the person will be a witness to or actually take on a role in a gospel story. With each meditation the person is led to ponder life through questions and quiet. Consequently, they will be able to reflect on Jesus' words and actions and integrate them into their lives in a definite way. So often we hear but do not apply. These twenty meditations nudge the Christian to wrestle with the spoken truths and make the God-given applications.

What follows in the introduction are several "rules of thumb" that can help set the atmosphere for guided meditations. These take into consideration space, preparation prior to the meditation, your role in the meditation, and the necessary concluding process. With time you will become comfortable with this style of prayer and will be able to adapt it to fit your own needs. The most fundamental point, however, is to set a tone by which the participant can settle down and encounter God. God does take care of the rest!

Each meditation is approximately fifteen to twenty minutes. They are to be read by you or another capable reader. The length really depends on how long you allow for reflection, both within the meditation and following. Anyone new to this style may need more time to settle into quiet while you shorten the reflection time during the meditation. However, do not always assume this to be the case. With time you will be able to assess the group and to time things accordingly.

I hope you enjoy this book. I prayed each meditation several times in its preparation. I suggest that you pray the meditations yourself before guiding a group. It will help you to read the meditation with meaning, as if you are inviting the person to a place with which you are already familiar.

meditation guidelines

As you begin to use this book and lead prayer with guided imagery, there are some simple guidelines that you may want to adopt and adapt to your situation. Several suggestions follow.

space

Being comfortable in your space is very important. Participants of all ages like to lie down on the floor. Carpet, carpet-squares, blankets, and pillows can be used. Spreading out is key because if the pray-ers are too close to one another they will distract one another. Adults won't have a problem with giving each other room. However, the teenagers—especially the younger ones—will need to be encouraged to space out adequately.

If you are leading the meditations in a classroom setting, adapt as best you can. In any case, you can allow the participants to put their heads down on their desks. Don't worry about them falling asleep. Rely on the power of God's word to speak to them regardless of their level of consciousness, though anyone obviously sleeping should be gently wakened.

changing the environment

Changing the environment from what the group uses normally (e.g., desks, discussion tables) to an atmosphere more conducive to prayer can have a great effect. Turn out the lights, use candles and incense, and rearrange furniture that may be distracting.

Choose instrumental music to play in the background. Absolute silence is very hard on many novice pray-ers. Using instrumentals or music with nature sounds is always a help. Stay away from music that would cause the participants to think about the words in the song and not listen to the meditation.

preparation

If your group has never done a guided meditation before then you may want to offer a brief explanation and example. Tell them they will be following your voice through a story of scripture. Explain that they will be imagining a gospel scene and placing themselves there as witnesses or participants.

Read the short italicized introduction for each meditation. Also, practice a relaxation technique with the participants. A variation of a basic relaxation technique is included with each meditation. Allow them to get comfortable in their position before you begin.

the meditation

Each meditation begins with a settling in time. You may need more time for the settling period. It depends on what you have just been doing with the group. Younger teens have a harder time flipping gears and they are uncomfortable with the beginning parts. They will get use to it with time. Adults and older teens seem to adjust rapidly and will tell you what they need to do in order to settle into a meditation. Listen to their suggestions.

Each meditation is written in line by line phrases. Pacing is very crucial in a guided meditation. Do not rush these phrases. Take a full breath (inhale/exhale) in between each phrase. (Remember, they are imagining what you are saying.) Yes, allow time, but not so much that the participants go off daydreaming or have the opportunity to fall asleep.

There are several places in the meditation where a longer time for quiet is intended. The **bold type** indicates this part. Pause after these phrases for up to one minute (timed by saying three "Our Fathers" to yourself). Sometimes you may want it to be shorter or longer. You have to watch the group. If it is too long they will get restless, but if it is too short then they are rushing through the reflection time that is the most important piece of the meditation.

At the conclusion of each guided meditation you slowly bring them back to their reality of time and space. Again, don't rush this part. This is one of the best parts because they will be relaxed and want to savor what they experienced. Adults and older teens will appreciate the time to re-enter. The younger teens will typically sit-up quickly because they don't want to be the last one lying down or sitting with their eyes closed.

your role

You are the guide. Your job is to provide a safe space so that the participants feel comfortable entering into this different form of prayer. Prayer is simply talking to God. The pray-er needs to feel that you are respectful of their personal time with God. Try not to forcibly direct the meditation by insinuating your own reflections. Encourage relaxation and trust. Ask them to go with whatever happens for them. Assure them that God is in it all.

concluding process

Afterwards, I usually stay away from a general discussion. This has been the participant's private prayer, albeit with a large group. I don't usually like to share my intimate conversations with God. However, you may want to go around the group and ask the participants to share "how was it for you?" In describing the experience, not the content, they will invariably share invaluable information. It will help you to evaluate the experience for the next time. Also you will begin to learn what works and how to help them with the experience. Or, you may simply ask the participants how they pictured a specific character in the story or event. Any reflection they offer is good because it leads you to a better understanding of the group's spiritual life.

Sometimes, and especially with younger teenagers, you may wish to have them draw or journal how the experience was for them. Concrete actions of this kind help them to focus and it isn't quite as threatening as speaking in a group about their feelings or experience. Any type of concrete reflection of this kind can help them focus better on the essence of the meditation.

the early years
and the beginning
of the ministry

"My soul proclaims the greatness of the Lord;

my spirit rejoices in God my savior."

LUKE 1:46

announcement of the birth of Jesus

LK 1:26-38

"Hail Mary, full of grace." These words spoken by the angel Gabriel to Mary announce the birth of Jesus. This meditation will place you into the scene in the role of Mary: listening to the angel, responding and trying to understand. Get ready to . . .

Quiet yourself.

Relax.

Feel yourself just letting go of everything.

Breathe in.

Hold.

Breathe out.

Breathe in.

Hold.

Breathe out.

Let go.

Totally relax.

Breathe in.

Hold.

Breathe out.

Breathe in.

Hold.

Breathe out.

Imagine . . .

14

You are in your home.

You are a young girl.

Engaged to be married.

You are doing some housework.

Picture this in your mind.

See yourself doing chores.

Imagine your wedding.

Suddenly you feel a presence.

It is hard to describe.

You are not afraid but very calm and at peace.

Be with this feeling.

"Mary," you hear your name and look around.

You walk outside

      to see who is there.

"Mary, don't be afraid."

You see something in the yard.

Go over there.

The voice continues.

"Rejoice, Oh highly favored daughter.

The Lord is with you, blessed are you among women."

Listen to these words.

Repeat them in your mind.

What do they mean?

Could the voice be an angel?

You hear, "Don't be afraid, really.

God loves you.

You are his favorite.

You shall conceive and bear a son and give him the name Jesus.

Great will be his dignity and he will be called Son of the Most High.

The Lord God will give him the throne of David his father.

He will rule over the house of Jacob forever and his reign will be without end."

Answer, "How can this be since I do not know man?"

Hear the angel say, "The Holy Spirit will come upon you and the power of the Most High will overshadow you."

Be with these words.

What do they mean to you?

Then the angel tells you something amazing about your older relative.

"Elizabeth, your cousin, who was thought to be sterile, has conceived in her old age.

She is now in her sixth month,

> for nothing is impossible with God."

How are you feeling?

What do those last words really mean, "nothing is impossible with God?"

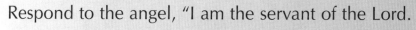

Respond to the angel, "I am the servant of the Lord.

Let it be done to me as you say."

Feel the angel leave you.

Repeat the angel's words to yourself.

"I am the Lord's servant.

Let it be done to me as you say."

What do these words mean for your life?

Breathe in,

let it be done.

Breathe out,

to me.

Breathe in,

let it be done.

Breathe out,

to me.

Let the words just come naturally as you continue to breathe.

Ask Jesus what meaning these words have for your own life.

Then slowly come back to this place.

What do you want to remember from this meditation?

What does God want you to remember from this meditation?

Open your eyes.

Slowly get up.

the visitation

LK 1:39-56

During this meditation you will have the privilege of being with Mary and Elizabeth, both expectant mothers. Listen closely to their greetings. Think about what their words mean. Ready yourself to ask them. Now . . .

Place yourself here.

Quiet.

Relax.

Let go of all the distractions.

Breathe in.

Hold.

Breathe out.

Breathe in.

Hold.

Breathe out.

Be still.

Relax.

Let all your worries fly away.

Breathe in.

Hold.

Breathe out.

Breathe in.

Hold.

Breathe out.

Imagine . . .

You are working in the yard.

Your neighbor Elizabeth is pregnant and cannot do these chores anymore.

A young lady comes up to the walkway.

She introduces herself as "Mary."

She says she is looking for her cousin, Elizabeth.

Lead Mary to her.

As you get close Mary calls out to her cousin.

Elizabeth looks up and immediately runs towards her.

She says in a loud voice,

"Blest are you among women and blest is the fruit of your
  womb.

But who am I that the mother of my Lord should come
    to me?

The moment your greeting sounded in my ears, the baby leapt in my womb for joy.

Blest is she who trusted that the Lord's words to her would be
    fulfilled."

You've never heard such a greeting before.

What do you think Elizabeth's words mean?

Then you hear Mary reply.

These words stay with you:

"My being proclaims the greatness of the Lord.

My spirit finds joy in God my savior.

For he has looked upon his servant in her lowliness.

All ages to come shall call me blessed."

Look again at Mary.

What is so special about her?

Now, listen to her continue,

"God who is mighty has done great things for me.

Holy is his name.

Can you relate to these words?

His mercy is from age to age,

>on those who fear him.

What do these words mean?

He has shown might with his arm.

He has confused the proud in their inmost thoughts.

He has deposed the mighty from their thrones,

>and raised the lowly to high places.

What kind of God is Mary describing?

The hungry he has given every good thing,

>while the rich he has sent empty away.

Do you know this God?

He has upheld Israel his servant,

>ever mindful of his mercy.

Even as he promised our ancestors, promised Abraham and

>Sarah and their descendants forever."

What has God promised you? What have you promised God?

The cousins go off to get Mary settled.

You go back to your work in the yard.

The scene and the words replay in your head.

What did you hear?

What did you learn?

What do you believe?

Both Mary and Elizabeth come out to the yard.

They bring you a drink.

Sit with them.

Ask them what their greetings meant.

Let them tell you their story.

Listen to them.

It is time to reenter this space.

Say good-bye for now.

Ask Jesus to lead your way into the rest of the day.

Say thank you.

Come back gently.

Open your eyes.

Remember.

Sit up.

the presentation in the temple

LK 2:36-40

In this meditation you are in the Temple area. A mother and father arrive with their infant baby. Come near them. Be yourself. Observe. Now . . .

Quiet yourself.

Relax.

Let go of the distractions.

Breathe in.

Hold.

Breathe out.

Breathe in.

Hold.

Breathe out.

Be still.

Relax.

Let all your worries fly away.

Breathe in.

Hold.

Breathe out.

Breathe in.

Hold.

Breathe out.

Imagine . . .

You are in the Temple courtyard.

It is busy there today.

You notice a young couple with a new baby.

It looks to you as if they are here to present the baby to the religious leaders.

Watch the couple.

An older lady approaches the couple.

You recognize her.

She is known as a prophetess of the Temple.

Her name is Anna.

She is highly respected and very holy.

She takes the baby from the mother's arms.

Anna catches you staring at her.

Anna comes towards you,

cradling the baby.

She hands the baby to you.

Take the child.

Look at the baby.

He is a boy.

Feel the baby in your arms.

Look up at Anna.

"This is the Promised One," she tells you.

"The One we have been waiting for."

What do her words mean to you?

Whisper softly in the baby's ear.

Tell the baby what is on your mind.

Anna reaches for the baby.

She takes the baby from your arms.

She turns and walks towards the parents.

Go to the parents.

Talk to them.

Tell them what this moment means to you.

Thank them.

Watch them walk away.

It is time to reenter this space.

Say good-bye for now.

Ask Jesus to lead your way into the rest of the day.

Say thank you.

Come back gently.

Open your eyes.

Remember.

Sit up.

Jesus is found in the temple

LK 2:41-51

Today you will take the role of a parent who is frantically looking for a lost son. In this meditation you will search out Jesus. What will you see and hear when you find him? It is time now, so . . .

Be still.

Let go of all the distractions.

Watch your problems fly away.

Breathe in.

Hold.

Breathe out.

Breathe in.

Hold.

Breathe out.

Breathe in.

Hold.

Breathe out.

Breathe in.

Hold.

Breathe out.

Let everything go.

Let your mind just be quiet.

If something comes into your mind
watch it fly away.

Imagine . . .

That you are either Joseph or Mary.

You are the parent of Jesus, the teenager.

What are you wearing?

What do you look like?

Picture yourself.

You are going back home.

You left Jerusalem yesterday after celebrating the Passover.

You are traveling with a large group.

You are walking with your friends while Jesus is walking with his friends.

What is it like to travel with friends and family, enjoying the journey, telling stories?

You haven't seen your son for a while.

But you are not concerned.

He is probably with his cousins and neighbors from the village.

One day passes into two.

You start the search for your son.

No one seems to have seen him lately.

As Jesus' parent, how do you feel when you cannot find him?

You reverse your steps and head back to Jerusalem.

What is it like to pass friends and family and to hear "we have not seen your son?"

The city is huge.

You look for him everywhere.

It has been three days.

You still have not found him.

Sit with this.

You decide to try the Temple.

Enter this sacred place.

There he is!

Watch him.

He is sitting with the teachers of the faith.

He is listening to them.

Asking them questions.

The folks around you whisper about how much he comprehends.

The questions he asks.

And the answers he gives.

Watch your son with the leaders.

Listen to the crowd talk about him.

Approach Jesus.

He does not seem concerned he has worried you.

Ask him, "Why have you treated us this way?

We have been worried, looking for you everywhere."

Jesus looks at you and replies, "But *why* were you looking for me?

Did you not know that I must be in my Father's house?"

What do these words mean?

How do you respond?

Jesus leaves with you.

You walk in silence.

Open the conversation.

Walk with Jesus, the boy.

Talk to him.

Ask him what it is like to be a teenager.

Tell him what it is like when you can't find him.

Be with him.

You rejoin the caravan heading for Nazareth.

How do you feel now?

It is time to come back into this space.

Say good-bye to Jesus.

Thank him.

Ask him to go with you into the rest of your day.

Be gentle with yourself.

Sit up slowly.

the baptism of Jesus

During this meditation you will be near the river Jordan. See John the Baptist. See Jesus. You will witness his baptism. So be present . . .

Settle yourself.

Relax.

Quiet.

Breathe in.

Hold.

Breathe out.

Breathe in.

Hold.

Breathe out.

Let go of all the distractions.

Simply relax.

See all of your problems just fly away.

Breathe in.

Hold.

Breathe out.

Breathe in.

Hold.

Breathe out.

You are near the water.

Hear its steady flow.

Watch its current, slow as it is.

Your mind is daydreaming.

You see a man in the water.

You learn his name is John the Baptist.

People are going up to him and he is dunking them into the river.

They are in line, waiting their turn.

Walk over towards the small crowd and watch.

Watch for awhile.

Do you want to approach John?

John suddenly just stops his routine.

A special man has reached the head of the line.

John engages the man in deep conversation.

You hear what they are saying:

"But I need *you* to baptize me," John says.

The other man is Jesus.

Jesus answers, "It is right for us to meet all the Law's demands—let it be so now."

Who is this man, Jesus?

What does he want?

Why is John hesitating?

John and Jesus head out into the water.

They are about waist deep.

Jesus leans into John's arms.

John baptizes him.

Watch the baptism.

Jesus comes out of the water.

The sky begins to change.

A dove appears over Jesus.

You hear a voice,

"This is my dearly loved Son, in whom I am well pleased."

Sit there and wonder what all this means.

Who is this Jesus?

Jesus moves on and the crowd disperses.

John goes along the shore.

Sit there, next to the water, and review all that you have seen.

Watch Jesus disappear on the horizon.

What do you want to do?

Talk to God about what you have witnessed.

Listen.

It is time to come back to this place.

Say good-bye to God.

Ask God to live in your heart.

Gently reenter this space.

Open your eyes.

Remember what just happened.

Jesus is tempted in the desert

MT 4:1-11

We all face temptations in life and Jesus did, too. During this meditation, you will walk in the desert, witness Jesus' being tempted by Satan, and think about where in life you are touched by temptations. It is time for you to allow the truth to speak. And now . . .

It is time to be quiet.

It is time to just relax.

Relax into this space.

Breathe in.

Hold.

Breathe out.

Breathe in.

Hold.

Breathe out.

Let go of all the distractions.

Simply relax.

Watch your problems just fly away.

Breathe in.

Hold.

Breathe out.

Breathe in.

Hold.

Breathe out

Imagine . . .

You are very hot.

You have been in the desert for a good deal of time.

You haven't had food or water.

You are tired and hungry.

And hot.

You look for a way out.

What is it like to be so totally alone?

How do you feel in this desert?

You see a figure on the mountainside.

It is Jesus.

Sit with him.

Another "person" approaches both of you.

It is Satan.

How do you react?

How does Jesus react?

Then Satan points to some stones,

and says to Jesus, "Tell these stones to turn into loaves of bread."

Think how simple it would be to get your hunger met this way.

What do you want Jesus to do?

Jesus looks at the tempter,

and says, " I do not live on bread alone but on the word of God."

What does it mean to live by God's words?

Walk on with Jesus.

Satan catches up with you again.

You are led to a cliff overlooking a city.

The tempter says, "Go ahead, jump, the angels of God will catch you."

Look down at the city.

Think about how easy it is to jump into things without thinking about the consequences.

When have you done something like that in the past?

Jesus replies, "Do not tempt God."

What does it mean to tempt God?

When have you tempted God?

Keep walking.

Up to a mountain's highest precipice.

Satan says to Jesus, "All you have to do is worship me and I will give you everything the world has to offer."

Satan says the same words to you.

What does the world offer you?

What are you willing to do in order to obtain it?

Jesus has beaten the tempter,

for now.

You turn to the tempter.

Tell the tempter to leave you alone.

Say with your whole heart,

"I will worship God and only God will I serve."

The tempter turns away and leaves you.

Reflect on what these words mean to you,

"I will worship God and only God will I serve."

It is time to leave this hot, desolate place.

It is time to come back to where you are.

What do you want to remember from your time in the desert?

When you are ready just open your eyes.

Look around.

Go gently as you sit up and remember your experience.

Jesus and the outcasts

MT 9:9-13

Often times Jesus ate with and talked to people that nobody else would. This meditation takes you to such a place and time. As you enter this place and time, think about people you know who are "outcasts" from the various peer groups that make up your world. How can you invite them to enter? Now . . .

Quiet yourself.

Be gentle as you go to that place in your heart.

Close your eyes.

Breathe in.

Hold.

Breathe out.

Breathe in.

Hold.

Breathe out.

Let go of everything.

See your problems just fly away.

Breathe in.

Hold.

Breathe out.

Breathe in.

Hold.

Breathe out.

Imagine . . .

You have been with Jesus and his friends for awhile.

There are a lot of different people who are with you.

It is a very diverse group of people.

Think of all the different people who are walking along with you.

Think of the differences among your own friends and peers.

You are passing the offices where taxes are collected.

A man named Matthew is standing in the archway.

He is one of *them*—a tax collector.

He invites Jesus to eat at his house.

Jesus says yes.

Unbelievable!

You are going to eat at the house of a person everyone despises.

How does that feel?

You come to his home.

The house is full of all kinds of people.

Some of the religious leaders are here.

You know they have come to "check up" on Jesus.

But what you really notice are the outcasts.

There are people here your parents would keep you from seeing.

There are people here your friends would tease or even shun for visiting.

What reason can Jesus have for eating with these people?

Why are you here?

One of the religious leaders asks these questions out loud.

What do you say?

How do you respond?

Jesus comes over to you.

He will answer.

He says, "Look, people who are in good health do not need a doctor; sick people do."

What does this mean?

What does this have to do with Matthew and the other tax collectors and outcasts?

Listen to Jesus' response.

The religious leaders leave.

You look back around at all the people who are in the room.

Are these people so bad?

How do you treat people who are outside of your circle?

In what ways do you need a doctor?

In what ways do you need Jesus?

Talk to him.

Now it is time to come back.

Enter into this space.

Be gentle.

Open your eyes.

What do you want to remember?

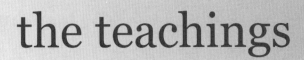

the teachings

> "YOU SHALL LOVE THE LORD, YOUR GOD,
>
> WITH ALL YOUR HEART,
>
> WITH ALL YOUR SOUL,
>
> AND WITH ALL YOUR MIND. . . .
>
> YOU SHALL LOVE YOUR NEIGHBOR AS YOURSELF."
>
> MATTHEW 22:37, 39

Jesus teaches us how to pray

MT 6:5-15

During this reflection, you will be alone with Jesus. Take this opportunity to be open and honest about your prayer life. Listen to Jesus as he teaches you how to pray. But first . . .

Come to the quiet.

Relax.

Enter gently into this reflection.

Breathe in.

Hold.

Breathe out.

Breathe in.

Hold.

Breathe out.

Be still.

Let go of all the distractions.

Watch your problems fly away.

Breathe in.

Hold.

Breathe out.

Breathe in.

Hold.

Breathe out.

Imagine . . .

You are with Jesus.

Just the two of you, no one else is around.

He is talking to you about many things.

Your mind wanders for a moment.

You think, "I am really here with him."

What does that feel like?

You hear Jesus say something that grabs your attention.

"Do not be a hypocrite."

Is Jesus calling you a hypocrite?

What does he mean?

He tells you, "I am not calling you a hypocrite.

What I am saying is do not become one."

He goes on,

"How do you pray?"

Ask Jesus how to pray.

Ask him to teach you.

He responds:

Our Father in heaven.

Who is God for you?

Holy is your name.

Is God's name holy for you or do you use it too freely?

Your kingdom come, your will be done.

Do you really want to know God's will?

On earth as it is in heaven.

How is God present to you through your day?

Give us today our daily bread.

Do you trust God to give you all that you need?

And forgive us the wrong we have done.

Ask God to forgive you all your sins.

As we forgive those who wrong us.

Will you forgive those who have hurt you?

Subject us not to temptation.

How can you keep from weakening?

But deliver us from the evil one.

Ask God to always be with you.

Look at Jesus sitting next to you.

He says, "This is how to pray."

Talk to him about your prayer life.

Tell him about your struggles with prayer.

Share your deepest desire with Jesus.

It is time to reenter this space.

Say good-bye for now.

Ask Jesus to lead your way into the rest of the day.

Say thank you.

Come back gently.

Open your eyes.

Remember.

Sit up.

the great commandment

What do we need to do to live a good life. Jesus' answer is love. Take this opportunity to reflect on how you live out this great commandment to love. Now . . .

Put yourself into this place.

Quiet yourself.

Relax.

Breathe in.

Hold.

Breathe out.

Breathe in.

Hold.

Breathe out.

Be still.

Relax.

Let all your worries fly away.

Breathe in.

Hold.

Breathe out.

Breathe in.

Hold.

Breathe out.

Imagine . . .

You are gathered with some religious people.

Many are "experts" in Jewish law.

Some of Jesus' friends are there too.

There is tension in the room.

The leaders have been grilling Jesus with questions.

Sit there.

Observe.

Participate.

One of the young lawyers in the group stands up.

He asks, "Jesus, which commandment of the law is the greatest?"

Without hesitation, Jesus answers,

> "You shall love the Lord your God
>
> with your whole heart,
>
> with your whole mind,
>
> with your whole soul.
>
> And you shall love your neighbor as yourself."

Listen to these words as if you are hearing them for the first time.

What place does God have in your life?

Who gets in the way of God?

How do you treat the people around you?

How do you treat yourself?

What does it really mean to love the way Jesus wants us to?

Look around the room.

See Jesus just sitting there.

Quiet.

The leaders have left.

Ask him how he wants you to love.

Ask him to show you the way.

Listen to him.

It is time to reenter this space.

Say good-bye for now.

Ask Jesus to lead your way into the rest of the day.

Say thank you.

Come back gently.

Open your eyes.

Remember.

Sit up.

the parable of the sower

MK 4:1-20

Jesus often teaches by parable. Sometimes his parables are hard to understand. His words are often surprising. Try to listen closely as you discover what his words mean for your life. To begin . . .

Enter into this space.

Be quiet.

Relax.

Enjoy the stillness.

Breathe in.

Hold.

Breathe out.

Breathe in.

Hold.

Breathe out.

Be still.

Relax.

Let all your worries fly away.

Breathe in.

Hold.

Breathe out.

Breathe in.

Hold.

Breathe out.

Imagine . . .

You are at a lake.

You are sitting on the shore.

Hundreds of others are with you.

Some have their feet in the water.

Jesus is out on the lake.

He is teaching from an anchored boat.

He can't come ashore or the crowd will smother him.

Why are you here to listen to Jesus?

He begins.

You have to strain to hear his words.

Your mind imagines what he is describing:

A man is sowing seeds onto the earth.

Some of the seeds fall by the roadside.

The birds come and eat them up.

Some of the seeds fall among the rocks.

Since there is not much soil they spring up very quickly.

The sun scorches them.

Some of the seeds fall among thorn bushes.

As the seeds begin to grow the thorns choke the life out of them.

They die, too.

And some of the seeds land on good soil.

When the seeds grow they produce a huge crop.

Jesus finishes the story.

He rows to the shore.

You walk towards him.

Sit with Jesus and his disciples.

One of the members of the group asks Jesus to explain the parable.

Listen to Jesus' explanation:

The man throwing the seed is delivering the message of God.

The roadside includes those people who hear the message but let it go in one ear and out the other.

It doesn't last.

The seed sown among the rocks represents those who hear the message

without hesitation.

They accept it.

But they have no real roots and it does not last.

Those are the people who give up when trouble arises.

Then there are the seeds thrown in the thorn bushes.

These are the people who hear the message, but the worries of this world
and the glamour of riches and all sorts of ambitions creep into their lives.

The world chokes the life out of the message of God.

As for the seed sown on good soil,

> they are the people who hear the message,

> accept it,

> and live the gospel message.

Jesus looks at you.

He asks, "Do you understand?"

Answer him.

He asks, "Which kind of person are you?"

Tell him.

It is time to reenter this space.

Say good-bye for now.

Ask Jesus to lead your way into the rest of the day.

Say thank you.

Come back gently.

Open your eyes.

Remember.

Sit up.

Jesus visits martha and mary

Imagine you are in the home of a friend. Cherish the friendship. Think about the relationship. Also do some honest soul-searching. Think about how your own life is going. So . . .

Enter into this space.

Quiet yourself.

Relax.

Breathe in.

Hold.

Breathe out.

Breathe in.

Hold.

Breathe out.

Be still.

Let go of all the distractions.

Watch your problems fly away.

Breathe in.

Hold.

Breathe out.

Breathe in.

Hold.

Breathe out.

Imagine . . .

You have been journeying with Jesus.

Going from town to town.

It has been exhausting.

You are going to get a break.

You finally arrive at Martha and Mary's home.

These are really good friends.

You are able to just relax.

Be with friends.

Good company.

Settle down.

Experience the feeling of calm wiping away the anxiety after a long trip.

Just sit back and watch everything happen.

There is nothing to think about or do.

Look around your circle.

These are your friends.

Mary is sitting with you.

Right next to Jesus.

They really get along well.

Martha is setting the table.

You can smell the good food coming from the kitchen.

She is such a good cook.

Just let yourself enjoy the moment.

Martha puts some snacks on the table.

You can tell that something is wrong.

Her face looks upset.

She turns to Jesus and says,

> "Why don't you tell Mary to get up and help me.

> I'm doing everything and she is just sitting there."

Look at Martha.

Hear her words.

How do they make you feel?

Jesus glances up at Martha, smiles and says,

> "Martha, you are right.

You are busy running around here and there.

You are worried about putting on a great dinner and making us feel comfortable.

But Mary has decided to sit and talk to us about our trip.

She has chosen the better part of hospitality.

You worry and are anxious about many things.

Leave her alone.

She is okay."

How is Martha responding to Jesus' words?

What happens next?

Jesus looks over at you.

He asks you how you feel about what he said.

He wonders how important it is for you to spend time with him.

Tell Jesus.

He asks you which person you are most like, Mary or Martha?

Talk to him.

Let yourself be with Jesus.

It is time to come back to this place.

Say good-bye to Jesus.

Thank him for this time together.

Ask him to go with you into the rest of your day.

Gently reenter.

Remember what you have just done.

Open your eyes.

Sit up slowly.

the prodigal son

LK 15:11-32

This meditation places you in the scene of Jesus' famous para-ble. A parable is a story that teaches a religious lesson with a surprising twist. Allow yourself to picture Jesus' story and to sit with what it means for you. Now . . .

Place yourself into this space.

Relax.

Quiet down.

Enjoy the silence.

Breathe in.

Hold.

Breathe out.

Breathe in.

Hold.

Breathe out.

Totally relax.

Go to that safe place in your mind's eye.

That place where you can just be.

Where no one can find you, disrupt you.

Where you can be with your thoughts.

Imagine . . .

Come to the teacher again.

He is there.

It is a beautiful day and the sun is shining.

You have been following the teacher around to various parts of the region.

Your friends are next to you as you sit listening to him.

It is fascinating.

He begins to tell a story.

Picture the scene.

He tells you to imagine everything he says.

Two sons.

The younger one decides he wants his inheritance.

Now.

So the father gives this son what he would eventually inherit.

The son packs up all his belongings and leaves for the city.

Imagine doing this.

The son loves city life.

He loves the lights, fast pace, action.

He goes to bars, stays out all hours, and parties very hard.

Eventually, the son spends everything he inherited.

He is wiped out.

His money is gone.

He finds himself on the streets without a place to live, or food to eat.

He looks for a job.

He becomes a laborer on a landowner's farm.

He is spent.

He has to feed his hunger with food intended for the pigs.

Imagine eating and sleeping in a pig's trough.

He is lying there hungry.

He thinks of home.

He thinks of his bed,

      the warmth,

      the food,

      the security.

He makes a decision.

He will go back home and ask his dad to take him back.

He will work for his dad like a hired hand.

His dad treats laborers better than this landowner.

He begins the trip back home.

He wonders if he will be accepted.

What is that journey home like?

The younger son is almost there.

Down the road his father sees him coming.

The son sees his father.

How do they feel?

The father runs back into the house and announces,

      "Prepare for a welcome home party!"

He goes back outside.

He runs to his son.

His arms outstretched.

Tears are running down his face.

They hug.

Watch the scene unfold.

Watch as the son asks for forgiveness.

Watch the father respond with unconditional love.

Imagine the preparations that are being made for the party.

Watch as the older son comes home from work.

He arrives in the midst of the commotion.

He asks one of the workmen, "What is going on?"

"Your brother has come home and your dad is so happy that he is throwing a party."

"What?" the son replies,

> "For my brother who took off with dad's money and left me to take care of everything?"

He refuses to go into the house.

He is very angry.

Watch the older son, how would it feel to be him?

The father sees his older son outside.

He goes out to talk to him.

The father says to him, "Isn't it great that your brother is back?"

His older son moans, "You really aren't taking him back are you?"

"He left us, remember?

Remember the pain,

the hurt,

the anger?

How can you just forget all that? I'm the one who stayed.

But, you've never thrown me such an extravagant party!"

Listen to the conversation between father and son.

What do their facial expressions reveal?

The father looks into the son's eyes.

He replies, "You are right, it was very painful when your brother left.

But he is back now and I want to rejoice that he finally came to his senses.

Listen, I know you have always been there for me— everything I own is yours.

Don't ever forget that.

I haven't forgotten.

But we have to celebrate and rejoice.

This brother of yours was dead and he has come back to life.

He was lost and is found."

What does it mean to say that the younger brother was dead?

Jesus calls you back from the story.

He looks at you.

You look at him.

He asks you, "Which son is more like you?"

Answer him.

Talk to him about the story.

Stay in the moment.

It is time to reenter this space.

Say good-bye for now.

Ask Jesus to lead your way into the rest of the day.

Say thank you.

Come back gently.

Open your eyes.

Remember.

Sit up.

the widow's mite

During this reflection you will be in the synagogue watching a scene unfold. You will learn what true generosity is all about and have a chance to talk to Jesus about it. So . . .

Relax.

Place yourself into this space.

Just quiet yourself.

Breathe in.

Hold.

Breathe out.

Breathe in.

Hold.

Breathe out.

Be still.

Relax.

Let all your worries fly away.

Breathe in.

Hold.

Breathe out.

Breathe in.

Hold.

Breathe out.

Imagine . . .

You are sitting in the synagogue.

You are quiet for prayer.

Jesus is in the synagogue, too.

You figure that he is praying.

He sits in front of you.

You notice other people coming in and out.

Just relax into this scene.

People are going over to the offertory basket.

You notice the well-dressed people examining their money.

Sometimes it is a large amount.

Then they throw it in.

You really don't think much of it.

It is part of the ritual.

Then you notice this little old lady.

Her gray hair is pulled back from her face.

She is bent over.

Leaning on each chair as she goes to the front.

She is moving slowly.

She is not dressed well:

      simple,

      clean,

      but poor.

She seems determined.

Watch her as she makes her way to the front.

She throws a few coins into the basket.

Jesus turns around and says to you and the others,

      "She has put in more than all the rest.

They make contributions out of their surplus,

But she from her want has given what she could not afford.

She needs every penny to live on."

Look at the woman as she returns to her seat.

She looks you in the eye.

Who do you see?

Turn back to Jesus.

Ask him what his words mean.

Listen to him.

He asks you, "Do you give from your need or from your surplus?"

Answer him.

Ask him to tell you what he wants from you.

Be still.

It is time to reenter this space.

Say good-bye for now.

Ask Jesus to lead your way into the rest of the day.

Say thank you.

Come back gently.

Open your eyes.

Remember.

Sit up.

the woman caught in adultery

JN 8:1-11

This meditation takes you next to Jesus as he is confronted with a moral dilemma. Allow yourself to listen carefully and watch intensely as this drama unfolds and Jesus asks each of us, "Who are you to throw the first stone?" Prepare yourself . . .

Enter in this place.

Relax.

Sit quietly.

Breathe in.

Hold.

Breathe out.

Breathe in.

Hold.

Breathe out.

Be still.

Relax.

Let all your worries fly away.

Breathe in.

Hold.

Breathe out.

Breathe in.

Hold.

Breathe out.

Imagine . . .

Hear the sounds of city life.

Feel all the people surrounding Jesus.

You are there on the streets with Jesus.

You are listening to his teaching.

Imagine yourself there.

Some important men from the Temple come pushing through the crowd.

They are dragging a lady by both arms.

They push her in front of Jesus.

She falls at Jesus' feet.

Listen to the gossip of the crowd.

"This woman," they say, "was caught in the act of adultery.

The law tells us that we should stone her.

What do you think, Jesus?"

There is a pause.

People near you pick up stones.

They are eager.

Sit with this energy around you.

Look for Jesus.

He is bent down drawing in the sand.

Everyone is waiting.

Be with the waiting.

The crowd is restless.

The woman is just there, alone.

Look at her.

Jesus finally stops playing with the sand.

He looks up but does not stand up.

He is ready to speak.

You listen attentively.

Everybody quiets down.

He says, "Let the one among you who has never sinned throw the first stone."

He bends down again, drawing in the sand with his finger.

What do you think?

What do you feel as you watch him?

People around you toss their stones on the ground,

> shrug their shoulders,

> walk away.

The important men stomp away angrily.

Look at Jesus and the woman before him.

Jesus finally stands up.

He looks around.

He asks the lady, "Where did everyone go—did no one condemn you?"

The woman answers, "No one, sir."

Jesus looks into her eyes.

"Neither do I condemn you.

Go home and do not sin again."

Watch what happens.

How does the woman respond?

Jesus turns to you.

He tells you, "Look into your own life."

Do what Jesus says.

Examine your life.

Where have you sinned?

Where have you judged?

Tell Jesus.

Listen to his reply.

It is time to come back to this place.

Say good-bye.

Ask Jesus to enter your heart as you go into your day.

Tell him thank you.

Gently open your eyes.

Remember what you just experienced.

Slowly sit up.

last days
and new days

"PUT YOUR FINGER HERE AND SEE MY HANDS,

AND BRING YOUR HAND AND PUT IT INTO MY SIDE,

AND DO NOT BE UNBELIEVING, BUT BELIEVE."

JOHN 20:27

"you are the messiah"

MK 8:27-30

In this meditation you take the role of Jesus' first disciple, Peter. Jesus will ask you a simple question—"Who do you say that I am?—and you will have the opportunity to respond. Get ready . . .

Relax.

Enjoy the quiet.

Let go of everything.

Breathe in.

Hold.

Breathe out.

Breathe in.

Hold.

Breathe out.

Let go of all the distractions.

Simply relax.

Watch your problems just fly away.

Breathe in.

Hold.

Breathe out.

Breathe in.

Hold.

Breathe out

Imagine . . .

Sitting in your favorite place.

Wherever it is you relax.

Just picture yourself in that place.

Invite your friend Jesus into your space.

You have heard all about Jesus.

You have even walked with him.

Now it is just the two of you together.

Facing each other.

Sitting there.

Being.

He looks at you and simply asks,

"Who do people say that I am?"

Think about society at large. What do they believe about Jesus?

Think about your friends. What do they believe about Jesus?

Answer him.

He asks you, "Who do you say that I am?"

Look at Jesus.

Look into his eyes.

Now answer him.

Just take some time and talk to Jesus about who he is for you.

What does Jesus have to do with your life,

your doubts,

your fears,

your beliefs.

Jesus now wants to say something to you.

Listen to him.

If your mind wanders, gently bring it back.

Listen to Jesus.

It is time to say good-bye to Jesus for now.

Thank him for the time together.

Ask him to go with you in your heart.

Then gently bring yourself back to this place.

a woman anoints Jesus at bethany

MK 14:3-9

You are with Jesus. You are at supper. A woman comes to Jesus and you will have the opportunity to talk with her. So . . .

Enter into this place.

Relax.

Quiet down.

Let go of everything.

Breathe in.

Hold.

Breathe out.

Breathe in.

Hold.

Breathe out.

Be still.

Relax.

Let all your worries fly away.

Breathe in.

Hold.

Breathe out.

Breathe in.

Hold.

Breathe out.

You are sitting around the table with friends.

Smell the rich aroma of a home-cooked meal.

Enjoy the companionship.

Picture yourself there with your friends.

A woman who does not belong to your group enters the room.

She looks around and heads towards Jesus.

What is she doing here?

What does she have in her hands?

What does she want?

Watch her.

She has a bottle.

She opens it.

A wonderful perfume fills the air.

She lifts the bottle over Jesus' head.

She pours out the perfume on him.

She rubs it through his hair with her hands.

Why is she doing this?

What is Jesus' reaction?

Judas yells out,

"What is the point of such a waste of expensive perfume?

It could have been sold for over thirty dollars

and the money given to the poor."

Everyone else is whispering, gossiping.

The woman ignores all of you.

She continues to anoint Jesus' head with perfume.

Look at Jesus and the woman.

The woman finishes.

Jesus glances around the table.

He says, "Let her alone; why must you make her feel uncomfortable?

She has done a beautiful thing for me.

You have the poor with you always.

You can reach out to them whenever you like."

Reflect on these words.

How are they true?

Jesus continues,

"You will not always have me with you.

She has done all she could.

For she has anointed my body in preparation for burial.

I assure you that wherever the gospel is preached throughout the whole world,

this deed of hers will also be recounted,

as her memorial to me."

Sit back and wonder what these words mean.

Go up to the woman.

Ask her why she anointed Jesus.

What does she say?

Talk to her about her actions.

Listen to her.

It is time to reenter this space.

Say good-bye for now.

Ask Jesus to lead your way into the rest of the day.

Say thank you.

Come back gently.

Open your eyes.

Remember.

Sit up.

Jesus washes his disciples' feet

JN 13:1-15

Jesus' ministry is a model of service. So it is no wonder that at his Last Supper Jesus would perform the ultimate example of service for his disciples. Witness and participate in it. Get ready . . .

Relax.

Be comfortable.

Close your eyes.

Breathe in.

Hold.

Breathe out.

Breathe in.

Hold.

Breathe out.

Be still.

Let go of all the distractions.

Let your worries fly away.

Breathe in.

Hold.

Breathe out.

Breathe in.

Hold.

Breathe out.

You are in a very simple room.

Sitting at a table with food and friends.

Jesus is there.

Peter, John, and all the other apostles are there, too.

You are remembering the Passover together.

You are nervous about what will happen to Jesus during this festival.

Sit back and look around the table.

How does it feel to be with friends, feeling these mixed emotions?

Notice Jesus getting up.

He takes his cloak off,

     ties a towel around his waist.

He fills a bowl with water.

He walks over to Peter and kneels down.

Watch Peter's face and the interaction between the two of them as Jesus washes Peter's feet.

What seems to be happening?

What are you hearing?

How do you think Peter feels?

The next thing you know Jesus is picking up the bowl.

Follow him with your eyes, moving around the table.

He is coming towards you.

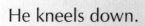

He kneels down.

Looks into your eyes.

Reaches for your foot.

Spend some time interacting with Jesus while he washes your feet.

Jesus stands up in front of you.

He moves to the person sitting next to you.

You are left there, in your seat, with your thoughts from your personal encounter with Jesus.

Name them.

How are you feeling?

Jesus finishes with the last person at the table.

He throws out the water.

Unties the towel.

Puts on his cloak.

Sits down at the table.

He takes some time to look around at the expressions of those who are there.

What is the mood of the group?

Jesus looks around at all of you.

He says: "Do you understand what I just did for you?"

You address me as 'Teacher' and 'Lord,'

And fittingly enough, for that is what I am.

But if I washed your feet—I who am Teacher and Lord—

Then you must wash each other's feet.

What I just did was to give you an example:

As I have done, so you must do."

Just relax and think about what Jesus' words mean for you.

It is time to come back to this space.

Just continue to lie there.

Gently roll your ankles.

Wiggle your fingers.

Shrug your shoulders.

Open your eyes.

Allow yourself time just to come back slowly.

Sit up, stretch, yawn.

Slowly.

peter denies Jesus

JN 18:15-18, 25-27

This reflection brings you near to the fire—figuratively and literally—listening to accusations and denials. Allow yourself to enter into the dialogue. Now . . .

Enter into this space.

Relax.

Quiet down.

Breathe in.

Hold.

Breathe out.

Breathe in.

Hold.

Breathe out.

Be still.

Relax.

Let all your worries fly away.

Breathe in.

Hold.

Breathe out.

Breathe in.

Hold.

Breathe out.

It is cold.

Someone has built a large open fire to keep warm.

You are standing next to the fire.

A lot of people do the same.

Your mind is exploding with thoughts.

Your friend, Jesus, was just arrested.

You and his followers came to this place where he is being kept.

The crowd is restless, hostile even.

What is it like to be in this place?

How are you feeling?

A woman glances over at Peter, a close friend of Jesus.

Stares at him.

She points at him.

She whispers something to the woman next to her.

She knows who Peter is.

What if she knows who you are?

Are you safe?

She walks over to Peter, her friend behind her.

She says, "You are one of his followers."

Peter jumps to his feet and denies it, "No, I am not."

Watch his expression.

Watch her reaction.

"Yes you are," she continues.

"I have seen you with that man they call Jesus."

Peter responds, "I am afraid you are mistaken."

Look at Peter's face.

She replies, "No, I am not, it is you."

"No," Peter says sternly, "Now get away from me."

He shoves her aside and walks away.

A rooster crows.

You look at Peter, stopped in his tracks.

He also heard the rooster.

You remember Jesus' words at dinner.

Jesus predicted that Peter would deny him three times before the rooster crowed.

None of you, including Peter, thought that it could ever happen.

Peter is one of Jesus' closest confidants.

What a terrible night this has been.

Let your mind replay the scene of Peter's denial.

Walk over to Peter.

Sit with him.

Listen to Peter as he tells you how he feels.

He asks you if you ever did something like this.

Answer him.

It is time to reenter this space.

Say good-bye for now.

Ask Jesus to lead your way into the rest of the day.

Say thank you.

Come back gently.

Open your eyes.

Remember.

Sit up.

doubting thomas

JN 20:24-29

Everyone knows the story of "Doubting" Thomas. He was the disciple not present to witness Jesus' appearance after his resurrection. Thomas would need physical proof before he would believe Jesus is alive. This reflection touches on the essence of faith. So . . .

Quiet your mind.

Be still.

Relax.

Breathe in.

Hold.

Breathe out.

Breathe in.

Hold.

Breathe out.

Be still.

Relax.

Let all your worries fly away.

Breathe in.

Hold.

Breathe out.

Breathe in.

Hold.

Breathe out.

Imagine . . .

You know a person named Thomas.

He was a follower of Jesus.

But Jesus has died.

He was, in fact, killed.

Be with your friend as he retells you the story of what happened to Jesus.

Listen to him.

Console him.

Go with him as he visits the other followers of Jesus.

Enter the house.

Hear the greetings.

Hear them tell you, "We have seen the Lord,

He is risen."

Your friend Thomas looks at you.

He is confused.

Look at him.

Think of a time when you felt really confused.

You didn't know what to think about a situation.

You were frightened.

How did it feel to be so unnerved?

Thomas says to the others,

"Unless I see in his own hands the mark of the nails and put my finger where the nails were,
and put my hand into his side, I will never believe."

Walk away with Thomas.

Listen to him as he talks about his feelings.

Then a week later you are with the disciples again.

The doors are shut and you are just talking about all the events.

You feel a presence.

Look up.

A man is standing there.

It is Jesus.

What is your reaction?

What is the reaction of the disciples?

What is Thomas' reaction?

He says to the group, "Peace be with you."

He turns to Thomas.

Jesus says, "Put your finger here—look, here are my hands.

Take your hand and put it in my side.

You must not doubt, but believe."

Thomas cries out, "My Lord and my God."

Jesus looks at him and says,
"Is it because you have seen me that you believe?"

Listen to Thomas' response.

How would you answer Jesus?

Jesus continues to talk to Thomas.

"Happy are those who have never seen me and yet believe."

Think about your own life.

What do you believe?

Do you need "seeing" proof like Thomas?

Tell Jesus.

Listen to his response to you.

It is time to reenter this space.

Say good-bye for now.

Ask Jesus to lead your way into the rest of the day.

Say thank you.

Come back gently.

Open your eyes.

Remember.

Sit up.

"it is the lord!"

JN 21:1-14

Picture yourself on your favorite sandy beach. You have the opportunity to rest on the beach during this meditation. It is a time for you to come to recognize Jesus and know yourself better in the breaking of the bread. Now . . .

Enter into the quiet.

Be still.

Close your eyes.

Relax.

Breathe in.

Hold.

Breathe out.

Breathe in.

Hold.

Breathe out.

Think of all your cares and worries.

Put them in a bottle.

Let them all slide into the bottle.

Take them to the river.

Put the bottle in the river.

Let them go.

Just totally relax.

Imagine . . .

Notice the fishing boat out on the water.

A man comes up next to you on the beach.

He yells out to the men on the boat,

"Have you caught anything?"

"Nothing," the fishermen on the boat reply.

The man shouts, "Try throwing your nets off the right side of the boat."

Why would they listen to this stranger?

Watch the men as they throw out their nets.

The nets start pulling down further into the water

They are full.

The nets do not seem strong enough for all the fish.

What is happening?

One of the fishermen looks towards the shore and yells,

"It is the Lord!"

The fisherman slips on some more clothes, for he was barely covered.

He jumps into the water.

Swims towards the shore.

The others start bringing the boat to shore.

Look at this person next to you.

What did the fisherman mean, "It is the Lord"?

Who *is* this man next to you?

Ask him.

He then asks you to help him build a fire.

Talk to him as you work.

Tell him what is going on in your own life.

Listen to what he has to say to you.

The other people join you.

There is fish on the fire and bread ready to eat.

Now you, too, recognize Jesus.

"Come and eat," Jesus tells you.

Sit down next to Jesus.

Jesus reaches over, takes some of the bread, blesses it, and breaks it.

He hands you a piece of bread.

He looks into your eyes.

Take it.

Eat it.

What does it mean to eat this bread?

How do you take this experience into your everyday life?

Listen to what Jesus has to say to you.

It is time to come back to this place.

Thank Jesus for this time together.

Ask Jesus to come into your heart.

Open your eyes.

Remember what you just experienced.

index of themes

This section includes some suggestions for possible lesson themes to go with each guided meditation. The meditations are categorized by themes.